Lerner SPORTS

— ULTIMATE SPORTS STATS —

PRO FOOTBALL
BY THE NUMBERS

Percy Leed

Lerner Publications ◆ Minneapolis

Statistics are accurate through the 2023 NFL season.

Copyright © 2025 by Lerner Publishing Group, Inc.

All rights reserved. International copyright secured. No part of this book may be reproduced, stored in a retrieval system, or transmitted in any form or by any means—electronic, mechanical, photocopying, recording, or otherwise—without the prior written permission of Lerner Publishing Group, Inc., except for the inclusion of brief quotations in an acknowledged review.

Lerner Publications Company
An imprint of Lerner Publishing Group, Inc.
241 First Avenue North
Minneapolis, MN 55401 USA

For reading levels and more information, look up this title at www.lernerbooks.com.

Main body text set in Adrianna.
Typeface provided by Chank.

Library of Congress Cataloging-in-Publication Data

Names: Leed, Percy, 1968- author.
Title: Pro football by the numbers / Percy Leed.
Description: Minneapolis : Lerner Publications, [2024] | Series: Lerner sports. Ultimate sports stats | "Statistics are through the 2023 NFL season"—t.p. verso. | Includes bibliographical references and index. | Audience: Ages 7–11 years | Audience: Grades 4–6 | Summary: "Who is the greatest quarterback in football? Which team has the best season record? Learn the answers to these questions and many more by exploring stats from the greatest football teams and players in history"— Provided by publisher.
Identifiers: LCCN 2023048909 (print) | LCCN 2023048910 (ebook) | ISBN 9798765625941 (lib. bdg.) | ISBN 9798765629871 (pbk.) | ISBN 9798765638163 (epub)
Subjects: LCSH: Football—Statistics—Juvenile literature. | Football—Records—Juvenile literature. | National Football League—Juvenile literature.
Classification: LCC GV955 .L44 2024 (print) | LCC GV955 (ebook) | DDC 796.332/640973—dc23/eng/20231128

LC record available at https://lccn.loc.gov/2023048909
LC ebook record available at https://lccn.loc.gov/2023048910

Manufactured in the United States of America
1-1010067-51928-3/6/2024

TABLE OF CONTENTS

INTRODUCTION
AMERICA'S FAVORITE SPORT 4

CHAPTER 1
PLAYER STATS 6

CHAPTER 2
TEAM STATS 18

CHAPTER 3
STATS ARE HERE TO STAY 24

Stats Matchup 28

Glossary 30

Learn More 31

Index 32

INTRODUCTION
AMERICA'S FAVORITE SPORT

Football is America's most popular sport. Fans have seen many changes to the National Football League (NFL) since it started in 1920. New rules, better equipment, and huge indoor stadiums have all changed the game. But one thing has stayed the same—the usefulness of statistics (stats).

Fans use stats to judge players and teams. Teams use stats to make decisions during games. What are football's greatest and most important stats? First, you should know a little about the sport's history.

CAMERAS RECORD EVERY MOMENT OF MODERN NFL GAMES.

PLATOON SYSTEM

In football's early years, most players stayed on the field all the time. They played offense, defense, and special teams. This was known as one-platoon football. One-platoon football is still used by many high school teams. But in college football and the NFL, each player focuses on one job.

PLAYERS WORE LESS EQUIPMENT IN FOOTBALL'S EARLY YEARS.

PLAYING GAMES

Until 1946, NFL teams played between 10 and 12 games each season. From 1947 to 1960, schedules were set at 12 games. Teams played 14-game schedules from 1961 to 1977. Beginning in 1978, the football season included 16 games. Then, in 2021, the NFL added a game to make the regular season 17 games. When comparing stats, keep in mind the number of games played each season.

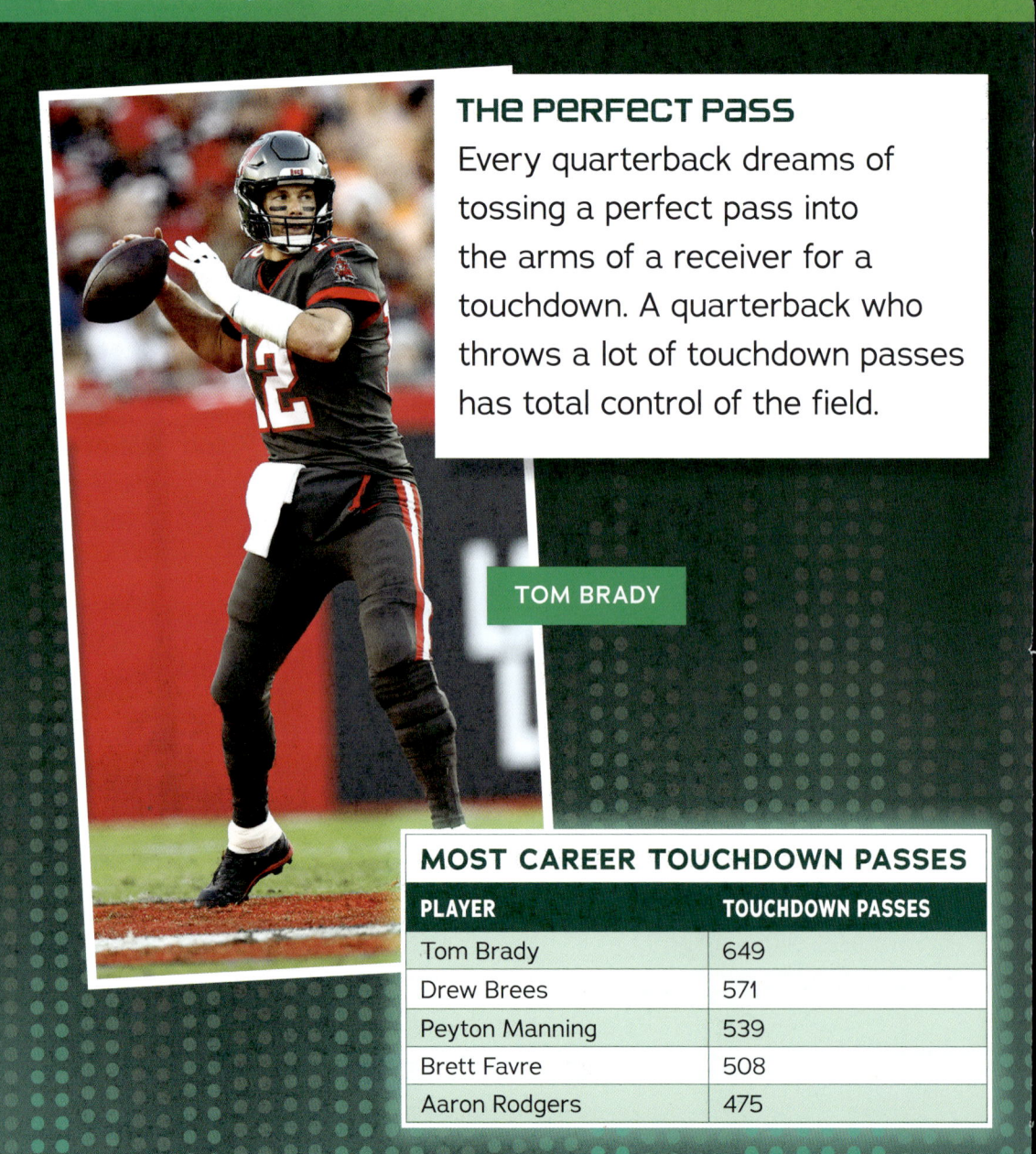

CHAPTER 1
PLAYER STATS

THE PERFECT PASS

Every quarterback dreams of tossing a perfect pass into the arms of a receiver for a touchdown. A quarterback who throws a lot of touchdown passes has total control of the field.

TOM BRADY

MOST CAREER TOUCHDOWN PASSES

PLAYER	TOUCHDOWN PASSES
Tom Brady	649
Drew Brees	571
Peyton Manning	539
Brett Favre	508
Aaron Rodgers	475

INTERCEPTION!

One record Brett Favre would rather not hold is most interceptions thrown. He ranks third in career passes thrown, so other teams had a lot of chances to intercept the ball. It's not unusual for great quarterbacks to throw a lot of interceptions. Of the top 20 leaders in interceptions thrown, 13 are in the Pro Football Hall of Fame.

MEKHI BLACKMON (*RIGHT*) INTERCEPTING A PASS

MOST CAREER INTERCEPTIONS THROWN

PLAYER	NUMBER OF INTERCEPTIONS THROWN
Brett Favre	336
George Blanda	277
John Hadl	268
Vinny Testaverde	267
Fran Tarkenton	266

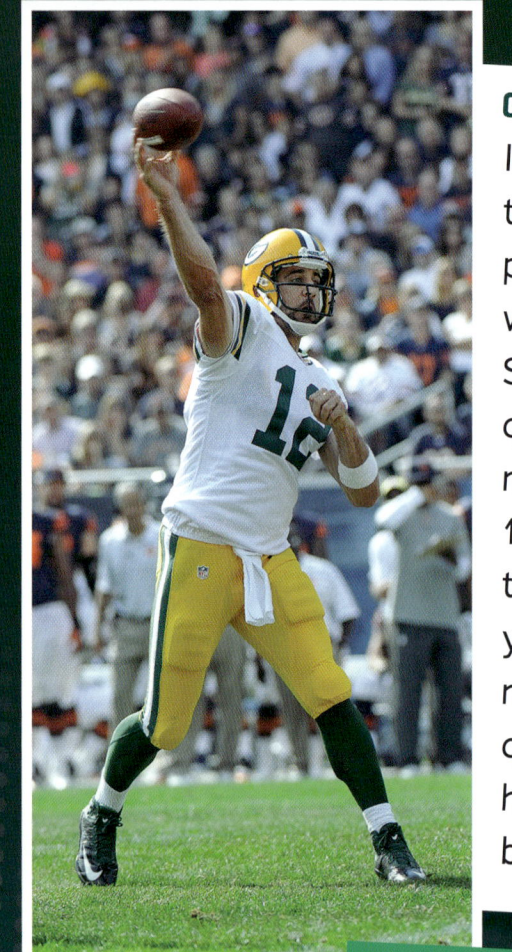

Great Rates

Imagine one quarterback threw 30 touchdown passes for the season while another threw 18. Suppose the 30-touchdown quarterback also threw more interceptions than the 18-touchdown quarterback threw. Who had the better year? Quarterback rating measures how well each quarterback played. The higher the rating, the better the season.

AARON RODGERS

BEST QUARTERBACK RATING FOR A SEASON

YEAR	PLAYER	TEAM	RATING
2011	Aaron Rodgers	Green Bay Packers	122.5
2020	Aaron Rodgers	Green Bay Packers	121.5
2004	Peyton Manning	Indianapolis Colts	121.1
2013	Nick Foles	Philadelphia Eagles	119.2
2019	Ryan Tannehill	Tennessee Titans	117.5

RUMBLING TO 1,000

For a running back, rushing for 1,000 yards in a season is the mark of a great year. Dallas Cowboys star Emmitt Smith did it 11 straight times on his way to more career rushing yards than anyone else. Only six teams have had two players reach at least 1,000 yards in a season.

EMMITT SMITH

TEAMS WITH TWO PLAYERS WHO GAINED 1,000 OR MORE RUSHING YARDS IN A SEASON

YEAR	TEAM	PLAYER	YARDS
2019	Baltimore Ravens	Lamar Jackson	1,206
		Mark Ingram	1,018
2009	Carolina Panthers	Jonathan Stewart	1,133
		DeAngelo Williams	1,117
2008	New York Giants	Brandon Jacobs	1,089
		Derrick Ward	1,025
2006	Atlanta Falcons	Warrick Dunn	1,140
		Michael Vick	1,039
1985	Cleveland Browns	Kevin Mack	1,104
		Earnest Byner	1,002
1976	Pittsburgh Steelers	Franco Harris	1,128
		Rocky Bleier	1,036
1972	Miami Dolphins	Larry Csonka	1,117
		Mercury Morris	1,000

JERRY RICE

Catching on Fast

As a child, Jerry Rice liked running on the dirt road in front of his house. Rice didn't know it at the time, but he was training to become the greatest NFL wide receiver ever. Rice holds nearly all the NFL's career receiving records.

MOST CAREER CATCHES

PLAYER	CATCHES
Jerry Rice	1,549
Larry Fitzgerald	1,432
Tony Gonzalez	1,325

MOST CAREER RECEIVING YARDS

PLAYER	YARDS
Jerry Rice	22,895
Larry Fitzgerald	17,492
Terrell Owens	15,934

MOST CAREER TOUCHDOWN CATCHES

PLAYER	TOUCHDOWNS
Jerry Rice	197
Randy Moss	156
Terrell Owens	153

GETTING THEIR KICKS

In 1938, NFL field goal kickers made less than 40 percent of their field goal attempts. In the 1960s, they made 56 percent. This stat has risen every decade since. Modern NFL kickers can make more than 80 percent of their field goal attempts.

DAVID AKERS (*TOP*)

HIGHEST CAREER FIELD GOAL PERCENTAGE (MINIMUM 100 ATTEMPTS)

PLAYER	PERCENTAGE
Justin Tucker	90.2
Harrison Butker	89.1
Eddy Pineiro	89.0

MOST FIELD GOALS MADE IN A SEASON

YEAR	PLAYER	FIELD GOALS
2011	David Akers	44
2021	Daniel Carlson	40
2005	Neil Rackers	40
2003	Jeff Wilkins	39
1999	Olindo Mare	39
2017	Robbie Gould	39

SACK THAT QUARTERBACK!

Deacon Jones was the leader of the 1960s Los Angeles Rams defensive line. Jones often tackled quarterbacks behind the line of scrimmage. But you won't find his name in the NFL record book for sacks. The sack was not an official stat until 1982.

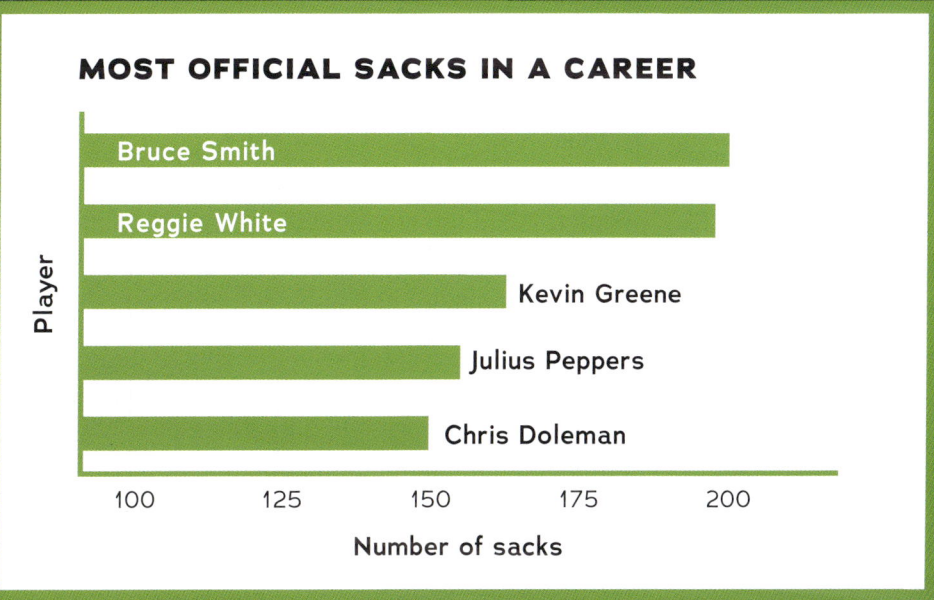

MOST OFFICIAL SACKS IN A GAME

- Derrick Thomas • 1990: 7
- Khalil Mack • 2023: 6
- Adrian Clayborn • 2017: 6
- Osi Umenyiora • 2007: 6
- Derrick Thomas • 1998: 6
- Fred Dean • 1983: 6

Player • Year / Number of Sacks

MOST OFFICIAL SACKS IN A CAREER

- Bruce Smith: ~200
- Reggie White: ~198
- Kevin Greene: ~160
- Julius Peppers: ~155
- Chris Doleman: ~150

Player / Number of sacks

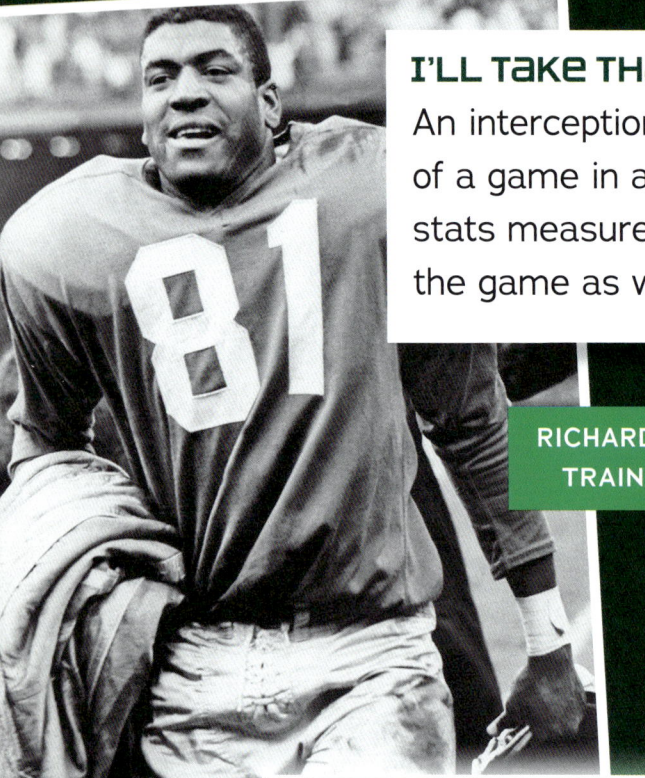

I'll Take That!

An interception can change the course of a game in an instant. Interception stats measure a player's knowledge of the game as well as their football skills.

RICHARD "NIGHT TRAIN" LANE

MOST INTERCEPTIONS CAUGHT IN A SEASON

YEAR	PLAYER	INTERCEPTIONS
1952	Richard "Night Train" Lane	14
1980	Lester Hayes	13
1950	Spec Sanders	13
1948	Dan Sandifer	13

MOST INTERCEPTIONS CAUGHT IN A CAREER

PLAYER	INTERCEPTIONS
Paul Krause	81
Emlen Tunnell	79
Rod Woodson	71
Richard "Night Train" Lane	68

MVP!

Each NFL season, sportswriters vote for the player they think is the most valuable to their team. Peyton Manning is the only player to win the Most Valuable Player (MVP) award with more than one team. Brett Favre is the only player to win it three years in a row.

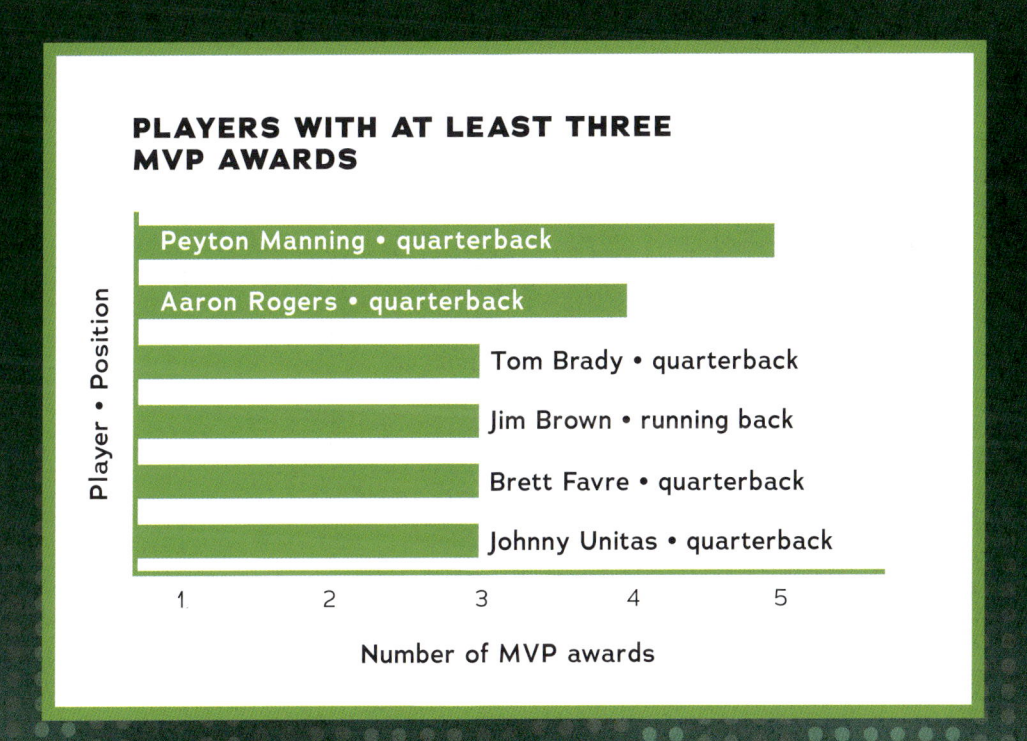

PLAYERS WITH AT LEAST THREE MVP AWARDS

Player • Position	Number of MVP awards
Peyton Manning • quarterback	5
Aaron Rogers • quarterback	4
Tom Brady • quarterback	3
Jim Brown • running back	3
Brett Favre • quarterback	3
Johnny Unitas • quarterback	3

Wait, What!?

Most fans agree that quarterback is the most important position in football. Baltimore Ravens quarterback Lamar Jackson won the NFL MVP award in 2023. It was the 11th year in a row that a quarterback won the award.

BRETT FAVRE (*TOP*)

ON THE FIELD

Brett Favre had many injuries during his time in the NFL. Yet he started every game at quarterback for 19 straight seasons. Favre finally missed games with a serious shoulder injury that ended his career. He retired with all-time NFL records for most passes completed, passing yards, and passing touchdowns.

MOST NFL GAMES STARTED	
PLAYER	**TOTAL GAMES**
Tom Brady	333
Brett Favre	298
Bruce Matthews	293
Drew Brees	286
Jerry Rice	284

TOUCHDOWN!

The ultimate goal of football is to drive the ball into the end zone. But it's not easy. Only 17 NFL players have scored five or more touchdowns in a game.

LADAINIAN TOMLINSON

MOST TOUCHDOWNS IN A GAME BY A PLAYER

YEAR	PLAYER	TEAM	TOUCHDOWNS
2020	Alvin Kamara	New Orleans Saints	6
1965	Gale Sayers	Chicago Bears	6
1951	Dub Jones	Cleveland Browns	6
14 players are tied with 5 touchdowns.			

Wait, What!?

On September 24, 2023, the Miami Dolphins beat the Denver Broncos 70–20. The Dolphins scored 10 touchdowns in the game. That tied them with two other teams for the NFL's single-game touchdown record.

CHAPTER 2
TEAM STATS

WINNING!

The New York Giants joined the NFL in 1925. Since then they've played 1,404 games, winning 721 of them. The Baltimore Ravens began in 1996 and have won 256 out of 451 games. How do you compare the two teams? Look at their all-time winning percentages. If a team wins half its games, the winning percentage is .500. The best teams have winning percentages above .500.

BALTIMORE RAVENS PLAYERS CELEBRATE A TOUCHDOWN.

BEST TEAM WINNING PERCENTAGES

TEAM	ALL-TIME RECORD	WINNING PERCENTAGE
Dallas Cowboys	562–413–6	.576
Green Bay Packers	799–598–38	.570
Baltimore Ravens	256–194–1	.569
New England Patriots	541–433–9	.555

Almost Perfect

The 1972 Miami Dolphins finished the regular season and playoffs unbeaten. No other team has been able to match them. The 2007 New England Patriots came close. They won all of their regular season games. But they lost the Super Bowl to the New York Giants.

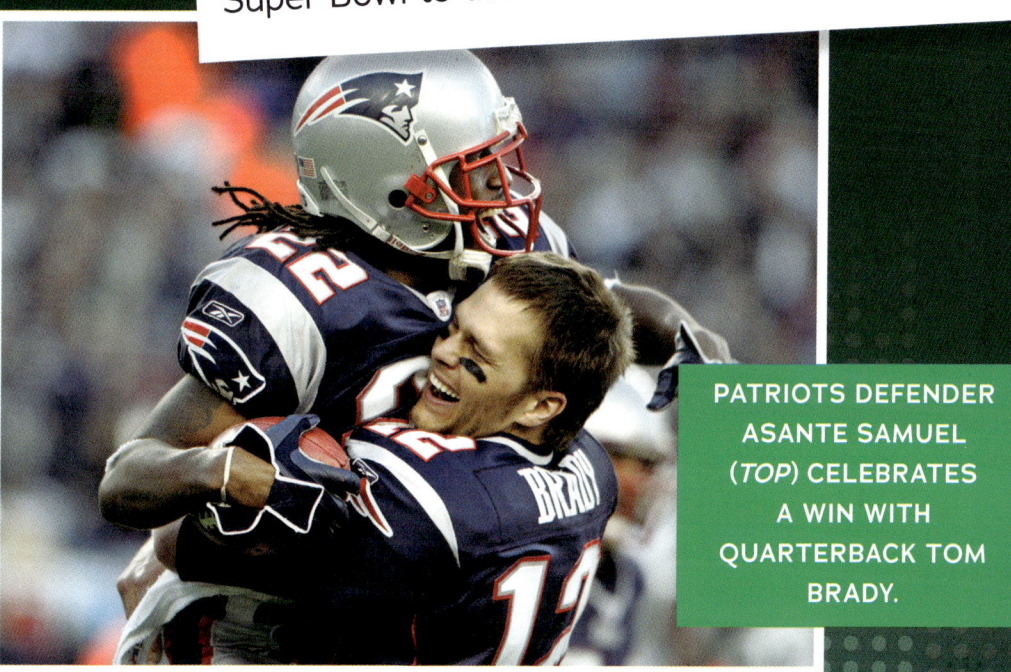

PATRIOTS DEFENDER ASANTE SAMUEL (*TOP*) CELEBRATES A WIN WITH QUARTERBACK TOM BRADY.

BEST NFL REGULAR SEASON RECORDS SINCE 1978

YEAR	TEAM	RECORD
2007	New England Patriots	16–0
2004	Pittsburgh Steelers	15–1
1998	Minnesota Vikings	15–1
1985	Chicago Bears	15–1

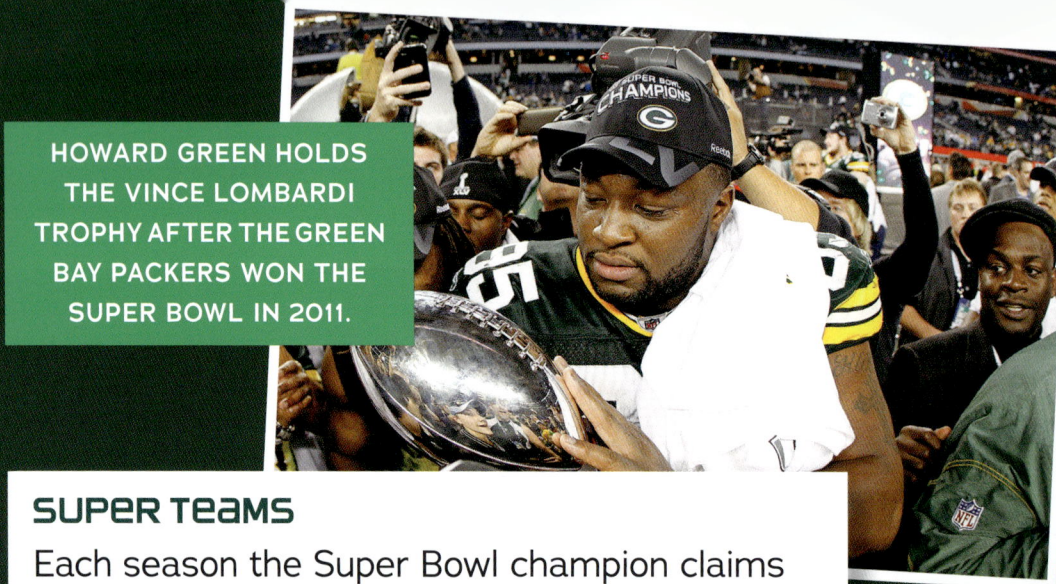

HOWARD GREEN HOLDS THE VINCE LOMBARDI TROPHY AFTER THE GREEN BAY PACKERS WON THE SUPER BOWL IN 2011.

Super Teams

Each season the Super Bowl champion claims the Vince Lombardi Trophy. Lombardi coached the Green Bay Packers to victory in the first two Super Bowls. In all, 20 teams have lifted the trophy, with 15 teams winning more than once.

TEAMS WITH THE MOST SUPER BOWL WINS

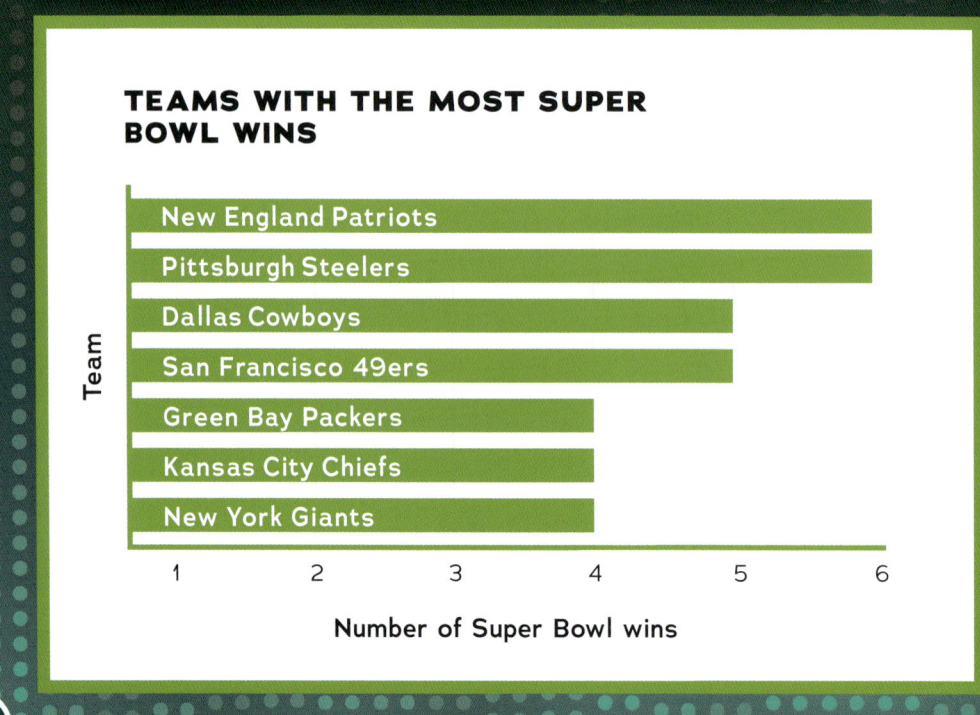

Team	Number of Super Bowl wins
New England Patriots	6
Pittsburgh Steelers	6
Dallas Cowboys	5
San Francisco 49ers	5
Green Bay Packers	4
Kansas City Chiefs	4
New York Giants	4

BEST COMEBACKS IN NFL PLAYOFF HISTORY

If your favorite team is trailing in a playoff game, don't give up hope! Plenty of teams have come from behind to win in the playoffs.

1957   The Detroit Lions trailed the San Francisco 49ers by 20 points in the third quarter. The Lions didn't have their starting quarterback. But backup Tobin Rote led his team to 24 straight points to win.

1993   The Houston Oilers built a 32-point third-quarter lead against Buffalo. Backup quarterback Frank Reich led the Bills to five straight touchdowns. They won with a field goal in overtime.

2003   The New York Giants led by 24 points against San Francisco. Then the Giants allowed the 49ers to score the game's final 25 points. San Francisco won by one point.

2014   The Indianapolis Colts trailed the Kansas City Chiefs by 28 points in the third quarter. That's when Colts quarterback Andrew Luck took over. Luck threw three touchdowns and scored another. The Colts pulled off the win, 45–44.

2023   The Los Angeles Chargers led the Jacksonville Jaguars 27–0 in the first half. But the Chargers could only score three points in the second half. The Jaguars came back to win, 31–30.

A BALTIMORE RAVENS DEFENDER TACKLES A NEW YORK JETS PLAYER IN 2000.

TO SCORE OR NOT TO SCORE

Fans love scoring. But a good defense wins championships. Since 2000, the NFL's highest-scoring team has only won the Super Bowl twice. But the team with the best defense has won the Super Bowl six times.

MOST TEAM POINTS SCORED IN A SEASON SINCE 2000

YEAR	TEAM	POINTS
2013	Denver Broncos	606
2007	New England Patriots	589
2018	Kansas City Chiefs	565

FEWEST TEAM POINTS ALLOWED IN A SEASON SINCE 2000

YEAR	TEAM	POINTS
2000	Baltimore Ravens	165
2000	Tennessee Titans	191
2002	Tampa Bay Buccaneers	196

HALL OF FAMERS

The NFL began in 1920 in Canton, Ohio. The Pro Football Hall of Fame is also in Canton. As of 2023, 371 people have been voted in. Every team has at least one player, coach, or team official in the NFL Hall of Fame.

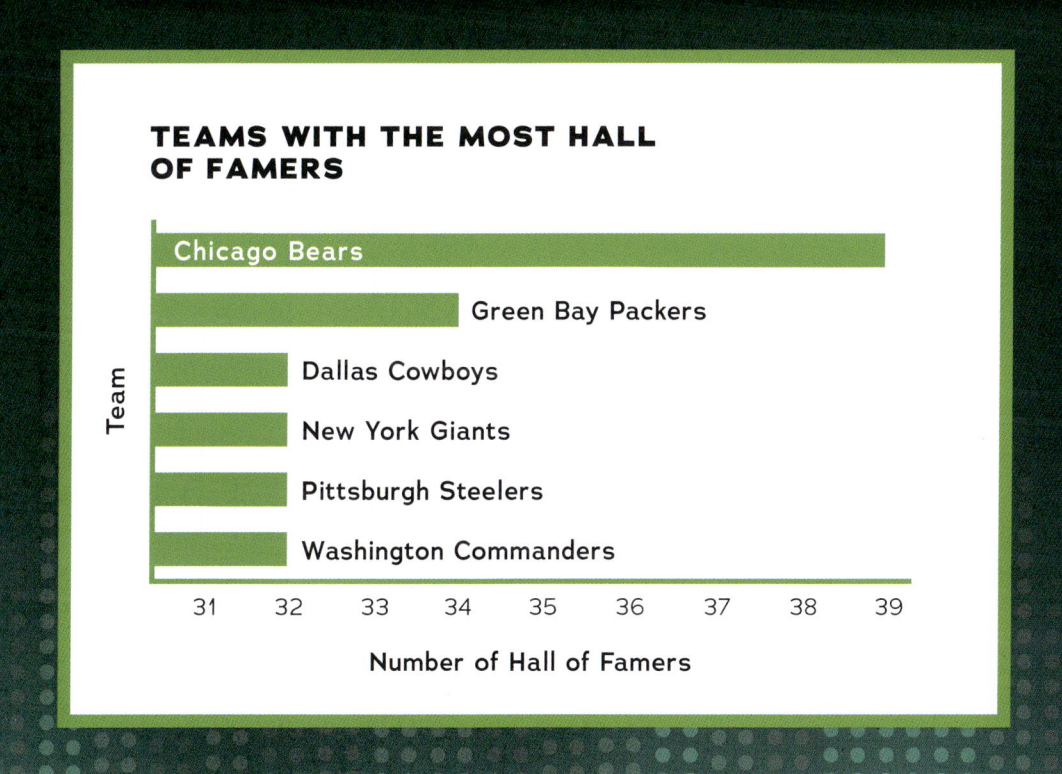

TEAMS WITH THE MOST HALL OF FAMERS

Team	Number of Hall of Famers
Chicago Bears	39
Green Bay Packers	36
Dallas Cowboys	33
New York Giants	34
Pittsburgh Steelers	32
Washington Commanders	32

WAIT, WHAT!?

It can take a long time for a player to join the Pro Football Hall of Fame. In 2023, Chuck Howley became a Hall of Famer for the Chicago Bears. He played for the Bears and Dallas Cowboys from 1958 to 1973.

CHAPTER 3
STATS ARE HERE TO STAY

THE BOX SCORE

If you look at a box score, you can relive the action of a football game. In 2023, the Kansas City Chiefs beat the Philadelphia Eagles in the Super Bowl, 38–35. On the next page, use the keys to read the Chiefs box score from the big game.

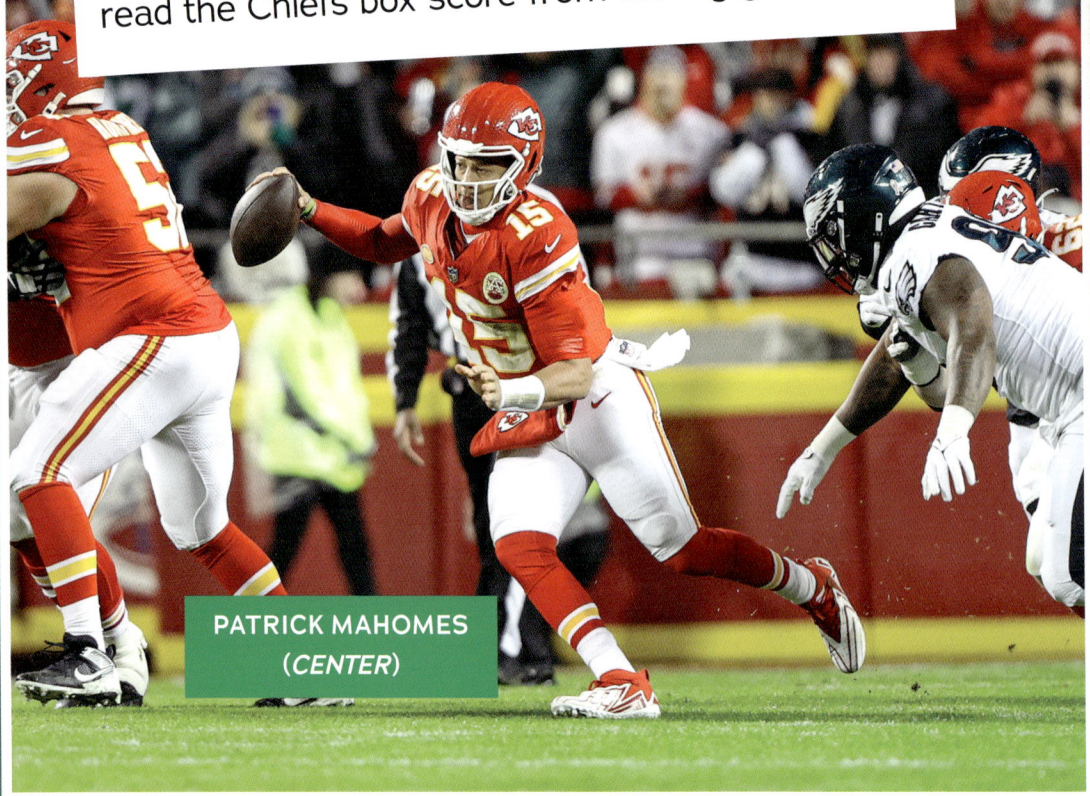

PATRICK MAHOMES
(*CENTER*)

PASSING KEY

ATT	= passing attempts
COMP	= passing completions
TD	= passing touchdowns
YDS	= passing yards

RUSHING KEY

ATT	= rush attempts
LNG	= longest rush
TD	= rushing touchdowns
YDS	= rush yards

RECEIVING KEY

REC	= receptions (catches)
TD	= receiving touchdowns
TGT	= targets (times thrown to)
YDS	= receiving yards

KANSAS CITY CHIEFS PASSING

PLAYER	COMP	ATT	YDS	TD
Patrick Mahomes	21	27	182	3

KANSAS CITY CHIEFS RUSHING

PLAYER	ATT	YDS	LNG	TD
Patrick Mahomes	5	44	26	0
Isiah Pacheco	15	76	24	1
Jerick McKinnon	4	34	14	0
Skyy Moore	1	4	4	0

KANSAS CITY CHIEFS RECEIVING

PLAYER	TGT	REC	YDS	TD
Jerick McKinnon	3	3	15	0
Skyy Moore	1	1	4	1
Travis Kelce	6	6	81	1
JuJu Smith-Schuster	9	7	53	0
Justin Watson	2	2	18	0
Noah Gray	1	1	6	0
Kadarius Toney	1	1	5	1
Jody Fortson	1	0	0	0
Marquez Valdes-Scantling	1	0	0	0

COACHES USE STATS DURING GAMES TO PLAN THEIR NEXT PLAYS.

STAT COMPARISON

Fans use stats to compare players and teams. Coaches look at stats to help make game plans. But nowhere in football are stats studied more closely than in judging talent.

The NFL Scouting Combine is an annual event where college players spend several days doing drills and tests. Athletes are tested on everything from how high they can jump to how quickly they can think. Coaches and scouts study their stats to help choose the players they want to draft.

Fantasy and the Future

Fantasy football is a popular game that adult fans play using the stats of NFL players. To play in a fantasy league, fans choose players to form their own teams. Teams are awarded points based on how well the players perform.

The NFL uses high-tech gear in pads, helmets, and footballs to keep track of stats. Fans and teams can see how fast a ball is thrown or how much force goes into a tackle. The NFL collects stats in new ways each season. How do you think teams and fans will use stats in the future?

FOOTBALL FANS WATCHING A GAME

STATS MATCHUP

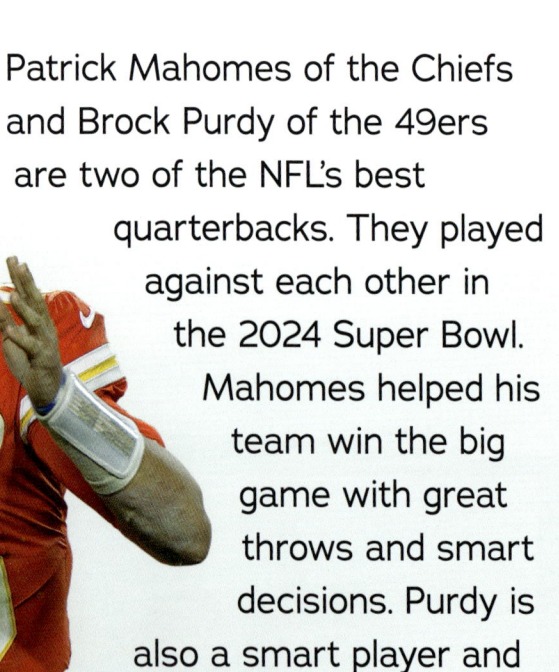

Patrick Mahomes of the Chiefs and Brock Purdy of the 49ers are two of the NFL's best quarterbacks. They played against each other in the 2024 Super Bowl. Mahomes helped his team win the big game with great throws and smart decisions. Purdy is also a smart player and an accurate passer.

PATRICK MAHOMES

PATRICK MAHOMES	
KANSAS CITY CHIEFS	
Pass completions	401
Pass attempts	597
Pass completion percentage	67.2
Passing yards	4,183
Passing touchdowns	27
Interceptions thrown	14
Quarterback rating	63.1
Yards rushing	389
Rushing touchdowns	0

Here are their stats for the 2023 regular season. Who is the more valuable quarterback? You decide.

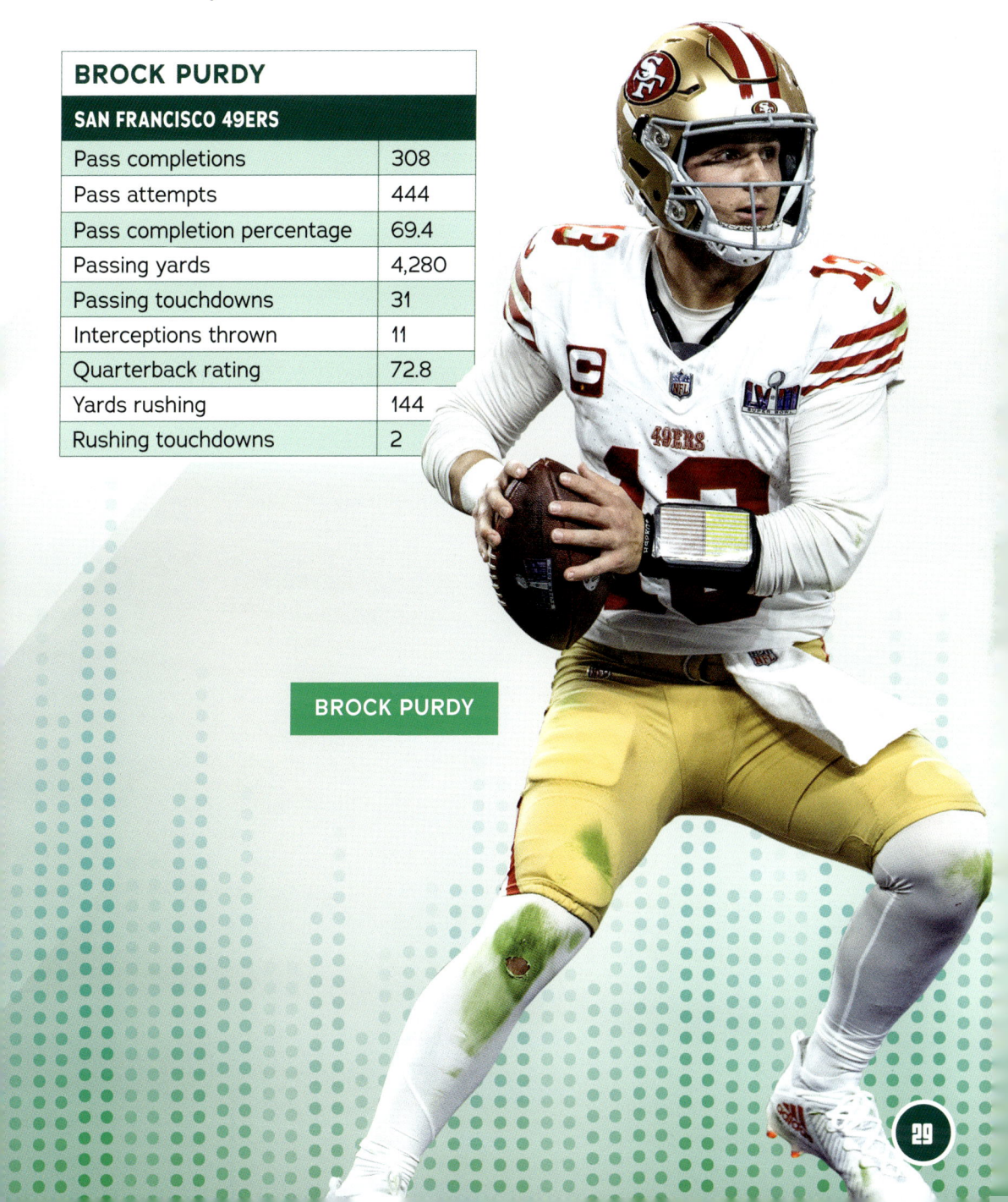

BROCK PURDY
SAN FRANCISCO 49ERS

Pass completions	308
Pass attempts	444
Pass completion percentage	69.4
Passing yards	4,280
Passing touchdowns	31
Interceptions thrown	11
Quarterback rating	72.8
Yards rushing	144
Rushing touchdowns	2

BROCK PURDY

GLOSSARY

defensive line: the players who line up on the defensive side of the line of scrimmage, rush the quarterback, and try to stop running plays

draft: when teams take turns choosing new players

end zone: the area at each end of a football field where players score touchdowns

field goal: a score of three points made by kicking the ball over the crossbar

interception: a pass caught by the defending team

line of scrimmage: an imaginary line that marks the position of the ball at the start of each play

pro: short for professional, taking part in an activity to make money

regular season: when all of the teams in a league play one another to determine playoff teams

sack: when a defender tackles the quarterback behind the line of scrimmage

special teams: the group of players on the field during kickoffs, punts, field goals, and points after touchdown

Learn More

American Football Facts for Kids
https://kids.kiddle.co/American_football

Anderson, Josh. *G.O.A.T. Football Defensive Linemen*. Minneapolis: Lerner Publications, 2024.

Blue, Tyler. *Legends of the NFL*. New York: Abbeville Kids, 2024.

Football: National Football League
https://www.ducksters.com/sports/national_football_league.php

Greenberg, Keith Elliot. *Patrick Mahomes vs. Peyton Manning: Who Would Win?* Minneapolis: Lerner Publications, 2024.

National Football League
https://www.nfl.com/

INDEX

comebacks, 21

fantasy football, 27

field goals, 12, 21

Hall of Fame, 7, 23

interceptions, 7–8, 14

Most Valuable Player (MVP), 15

quarterbacks, 6–8, 13, 15–16, 21

running backs, 9, 15

sacks, 13

Scouting Combine, 26

Super Bowl, 19–20, 22, 24

touchdowns, 6, 8, 11, 16–17, 21, 25

wide receivers, 11

winning percentage, 18

PHOTO ACKNOWLEDGMENTS

Image credits: Focus On Sport/Getty Images, pp. 4, 10, 22; AP Photo/Associated Press, p. 5; Douglas P. DeFelice/Getty Images, p. 6; Adam Bettcher/Getty Images, p. 7; David Banks/Stringer/Getty Images, p. 8; Mike Moore/Getty Images, p. 9; Norm Hall/Getty Images, p. 12; AP Photo/Preston Stroup, p. 14; Icon Sports Wire/Getty Images, p. 16; Mark Konezny/Getty Images, p. 17; Patrick Smith/Getty Images, p. 18; MediaNews Group/Boston Herald/Getty Images, p. 19; Kevin C. Cox/Getty Images, p. 20; Perry Knotts/Getty Images, p. 24; Erick W. Rasco/Getty Images, p. 26; Robert Deutschman/Getty Images, p. 27; AP Photo/Scott Boehm, p. 28; Lauren Leigh Bacho/Getty Images, p. 29.

Design elements: Ali Kahfi/Getty Images; sarayut Thaneerat/Getty Images.

Cover: AP Photo/Matt Rourke.